WHEN DID MAN FIRST GO TO SPACE?

HISTORY OF SPACE EXPLORATIONS ASTRONOMY FOR KIDS CHILDREN'S ASTRONOMY & SPACE BOOKS

BABY PROFESSOR
EDUCATION KIDS

Speedy Publishing LLC

40 E. Main St. #1156

Newark, DE 19711

www.speedypublishing.com

Copyright 2017

All Rights reserved. No part of this book may be reproduced or used in any way or form or by any means whether electronic or mechanical, this means that you cannot record or photocopy any material ideas or tips that are provided in this book

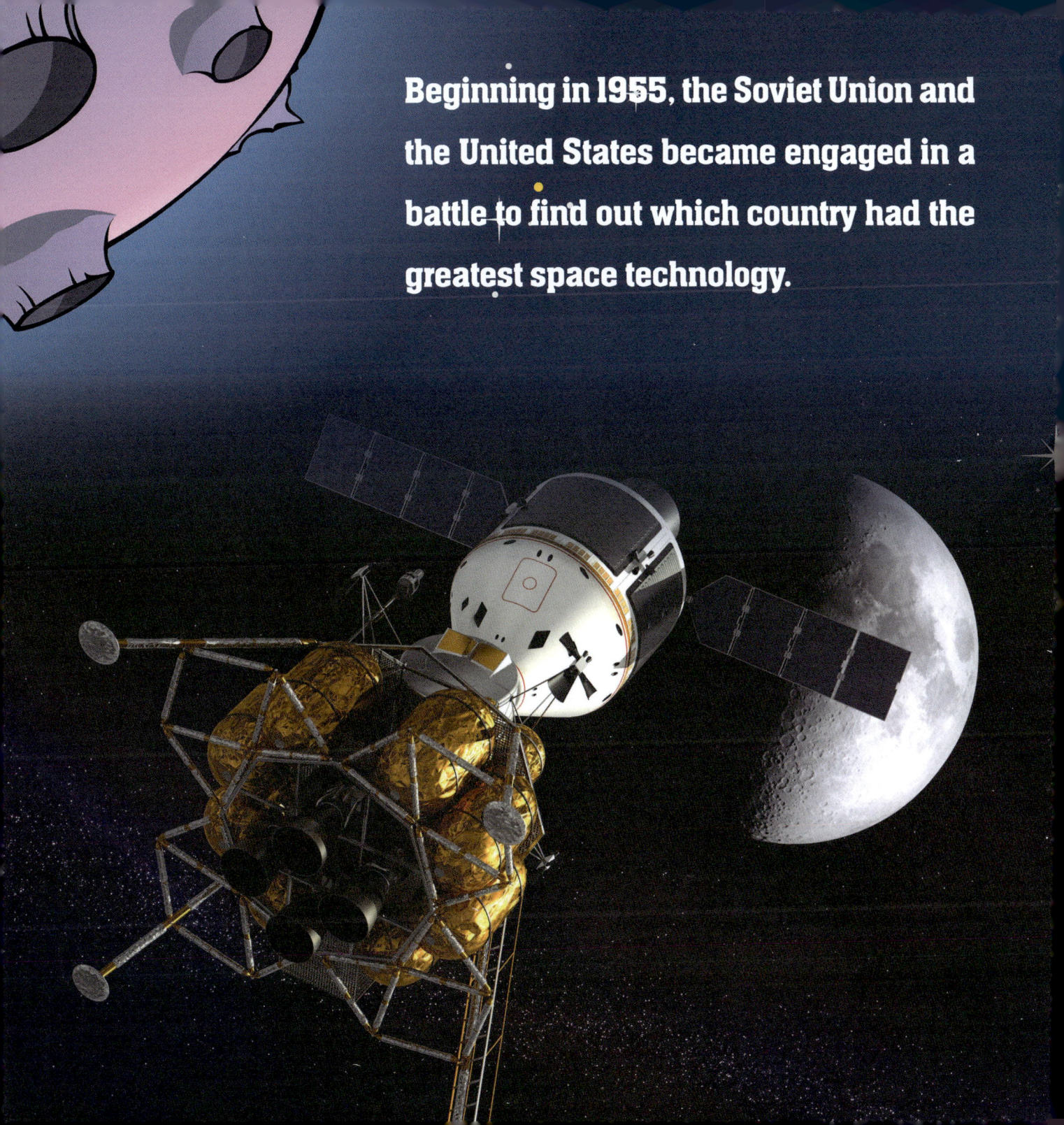

Beginning in 1955, the Soviet Union and the United States became engaged in a battle to find out which country had the greatest space technology.

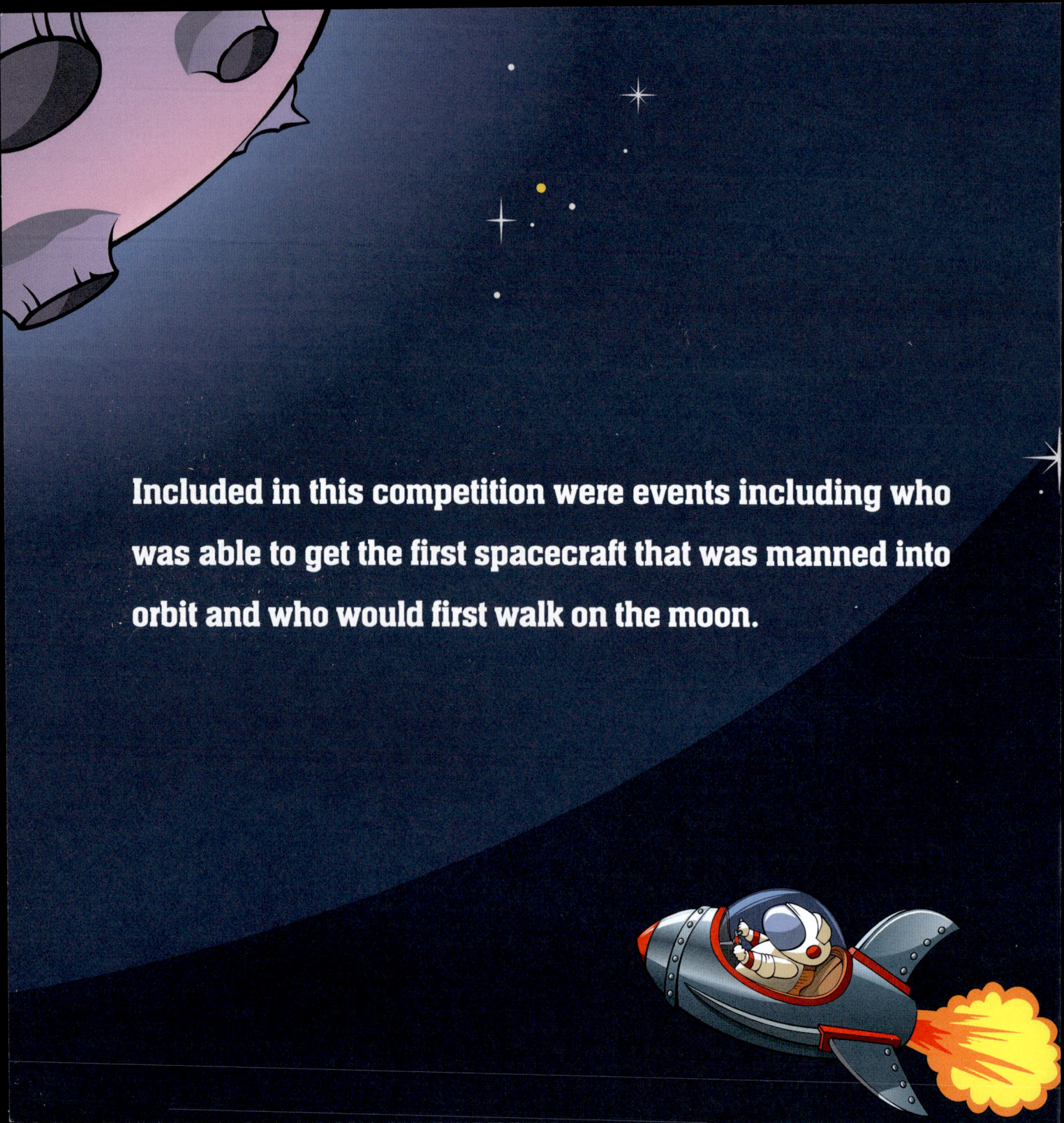

Included in this competition were events including who was able to get the first spacecraft that was manned into orbit and who would first walk on the moon.

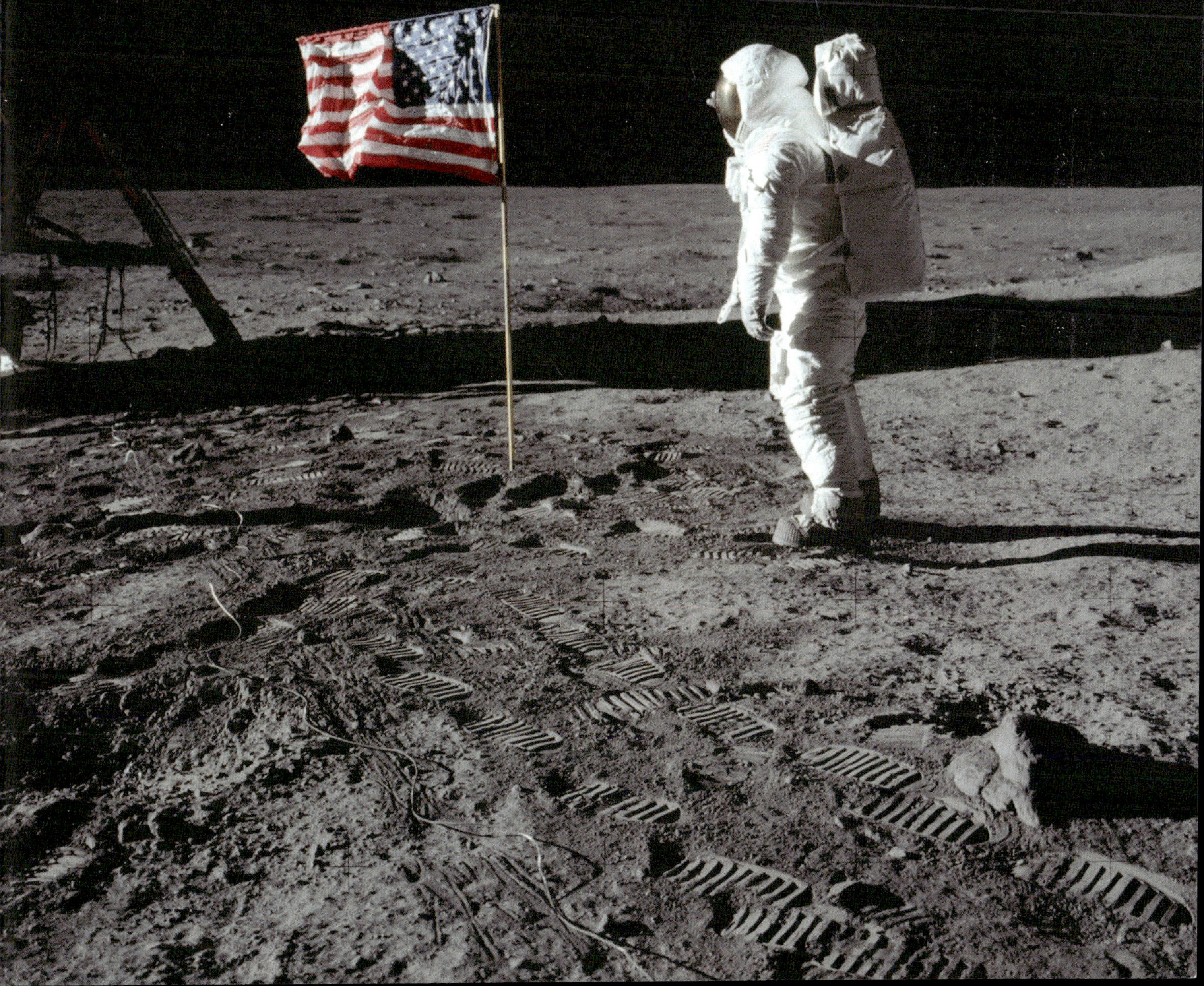

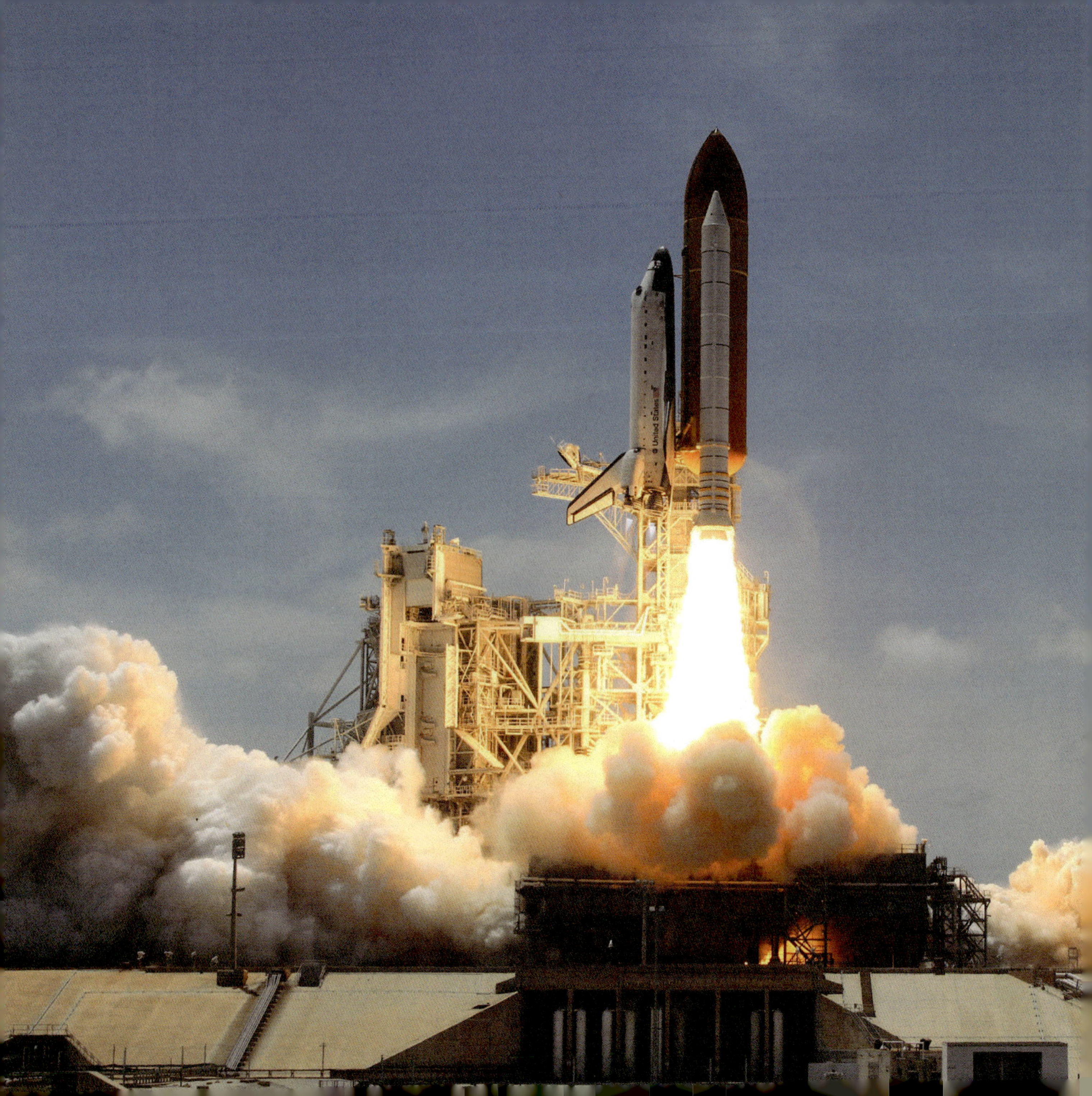
United States

This became known as the Space Race and was regarded as importance since it would show the world which country was known for having the best economic, technology, and science. Read further to learn more about the Space Race.

THE BEGINNING OF THE SPACE RACE

Following World War II both the Soviet Union and the United States came to realize just how important space research would be with the military forces. They had each started to recruit the greatest rocket scientists from Germany for

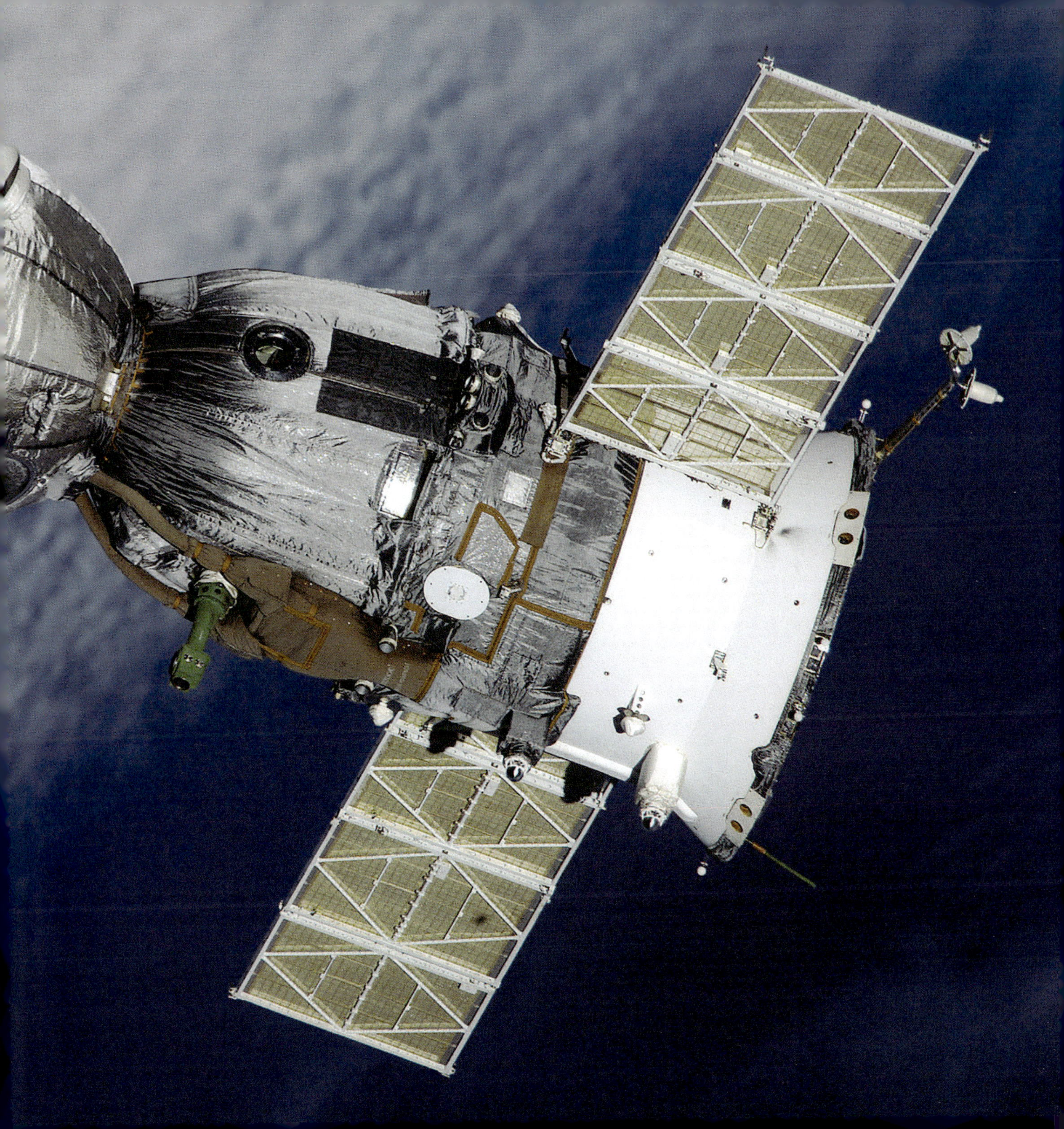

Sputnik I replica

The Race started in 1955 when both countries revealed they would be launching satellites into orbit in the near future. When the United States made their announcement, the Soviets took it as a challenge and proceeded to establish a commission whose purpose was to get a satellite into space before the US.

The Russians proceeded to send their first successful satellite into space on October 4, 1957. They had named it Sputnik I. This placed the Russians in the lead. Four months later, the Americans were successful in launching the first satellite into space. This satellite was named Explorer I.

Explorer 1

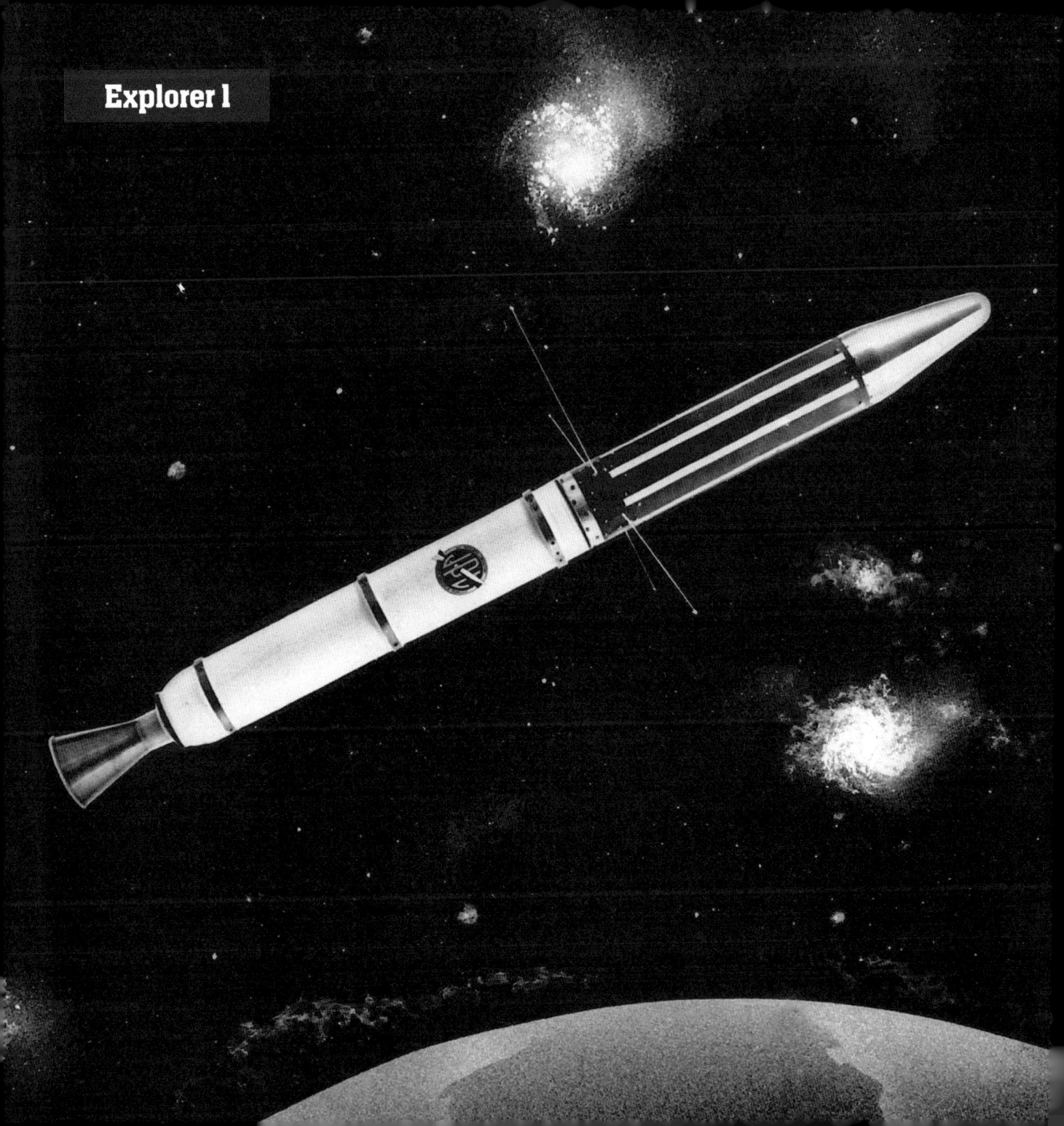

Dwight Eisenhower

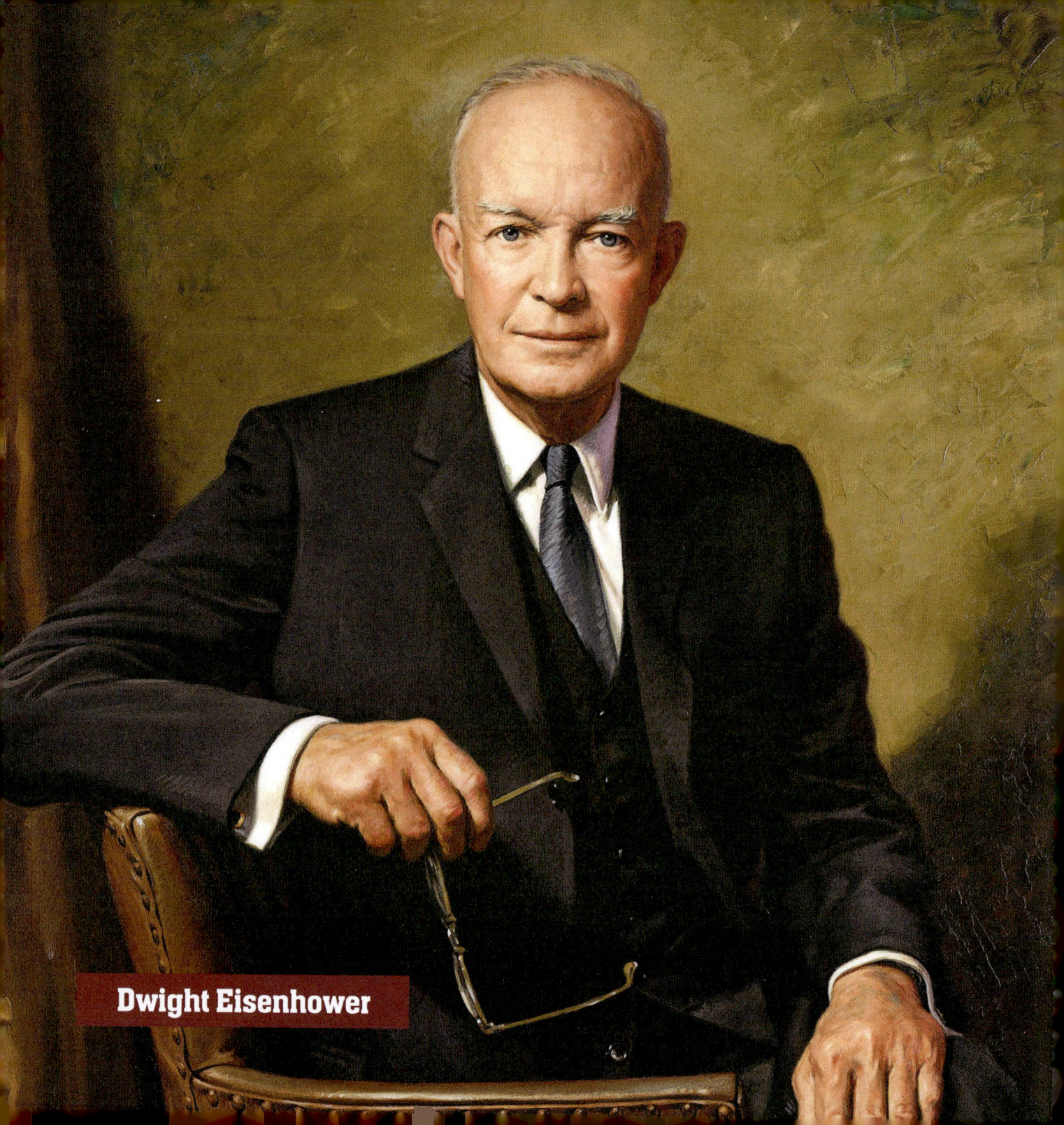

More than likely, the United States would have had the first spacecraft in orbit if they were allowed the use of military rockets at the beginning. Eisenhower, however, became worried that he would be known as a warmonger if the permitted use of these military rockets for space travel. He advised the scientists that they had to use research rockets.

ASTRONAUT OR COSMONAUT?

An astronaut is someone that is specially trained for travel in outer space. On board a spacecraft, they have various responsibilities. Normally there is a commander leading the mission, and a pilot. Some of the other positions include a science pilot, a mission specialist, a payload commander, and a flight engineer. The term astronaut means "star sailor".

Astronaut

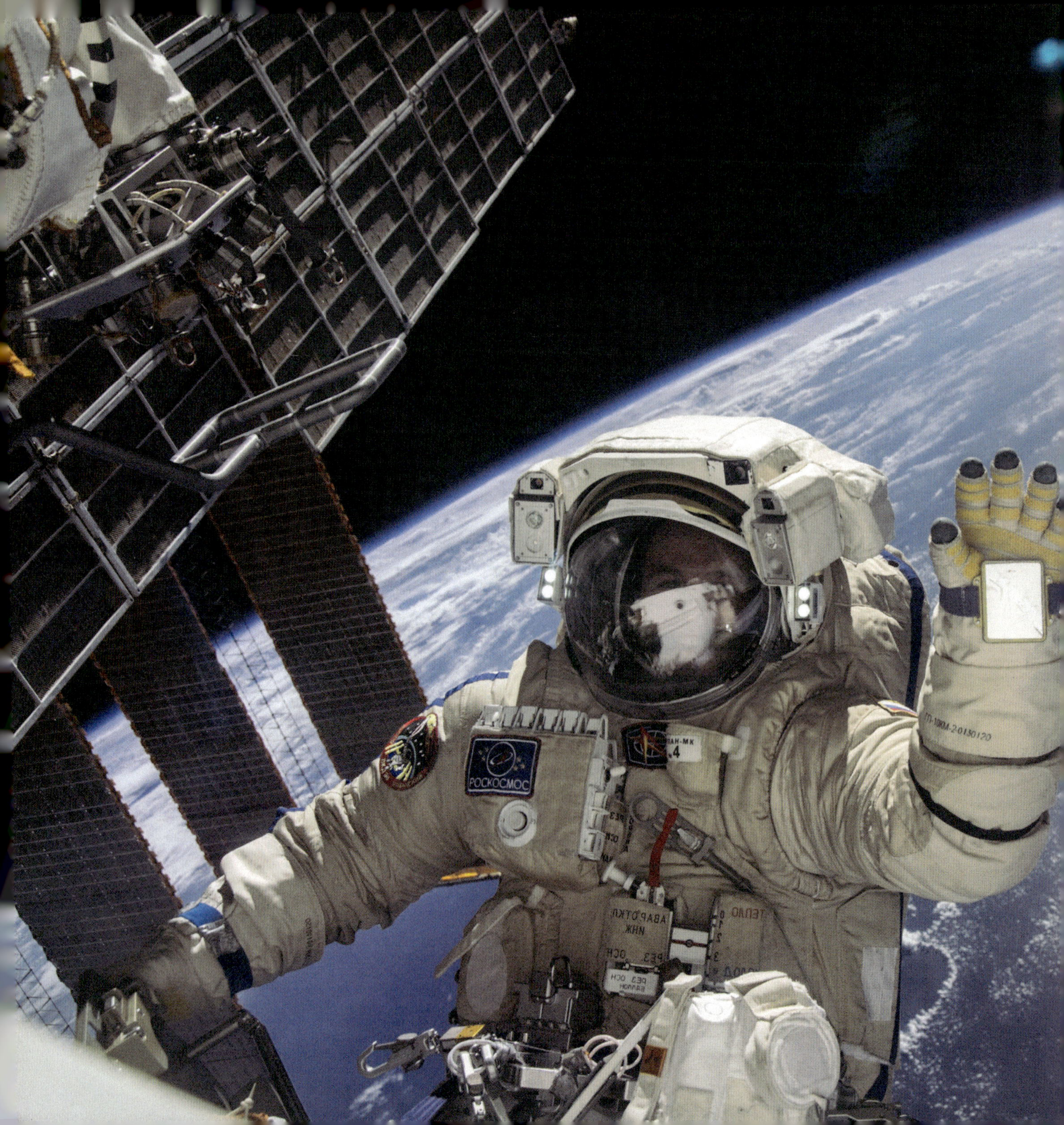
РОСКОСМОС

The Russians refer to their space pilots as cosmonauts, and they have to endure the same training for travel in outer space. The term cosmonaut means "sailors of the universe".

THE FIRST PERSON IN ORBIT

Again, the Soviets won this race. Yuri Gagarin, on April 12, 1961, took the honor of being the first person to orbit Earth in the spacecraft named Vostok I. The US then launched Freedom 7 three weeks later, and astronaut Alan Shepherd was the first American to enter space. However, this craft did not orbit Earth. On February 20, 1962, almost a year later, John Glenn became the first American to orbit the Earth on the spacecraft named Friendship 7.

Yuri Gagarin Monument

APOLLO
Moon

APOLLO

The Americans became embarrassed because they were losing the Space Race. President Kennedy went to congress in 1961 and told them he wanted the United States to be first at putting a man on the moon. He believed this was of importance to our country as well as the western world. The program known as Apollo Moon was then launched.

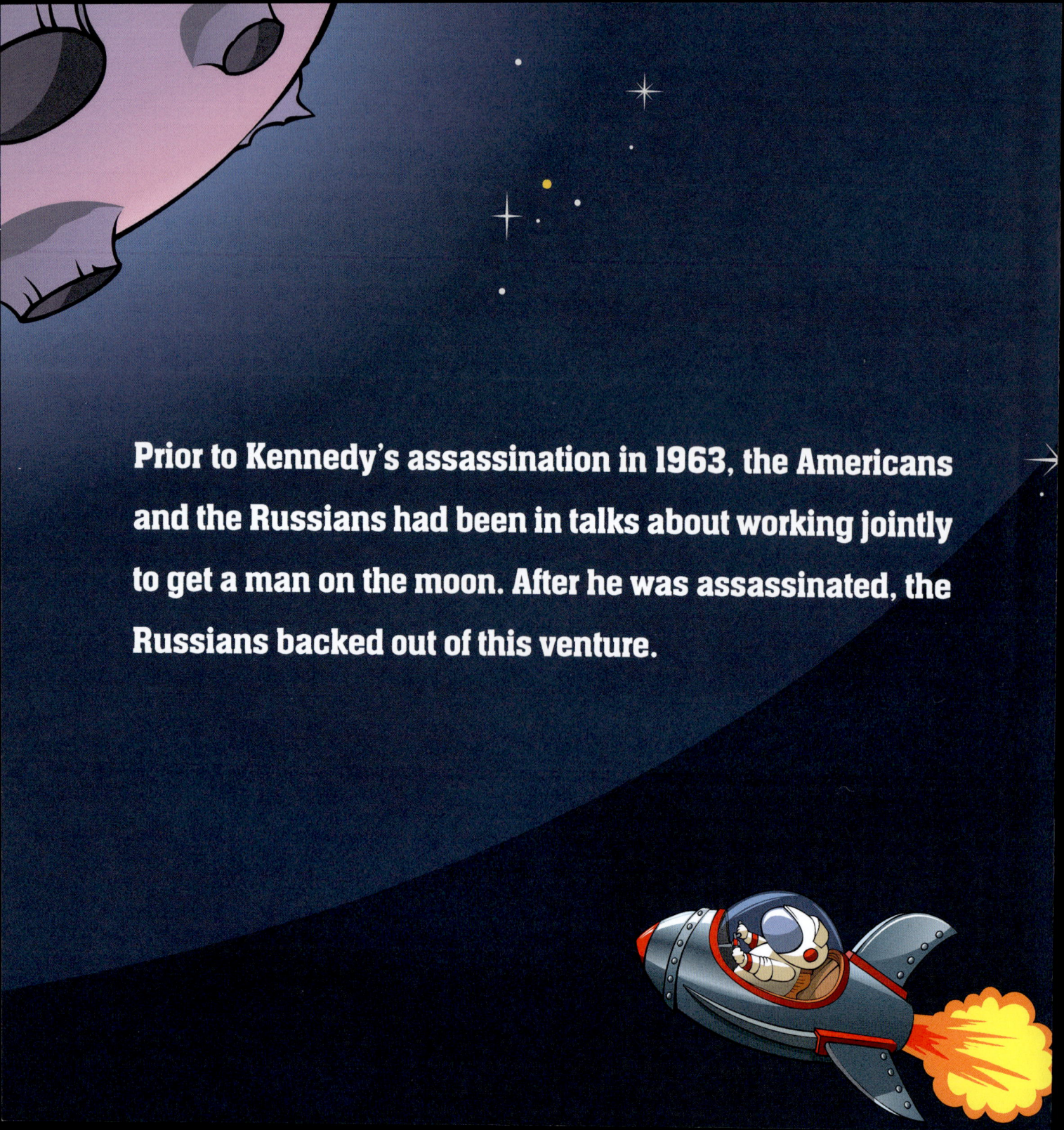

Prior to Kennedy's assassination in 1963, the Americans and the Russians had been in talks about working jointly to get a man on the moon. After he was assassinated, the Russians backed out of this venture.

Apollo

Gemini

GEMINI

The US then launched the Gemini program along with the Apollo program for developing technology to use on the Apollo. With the Gemini program, Americans spent a significant amount of time in orbit learning how the human body would react, they learned about changing the spacecraft's orbit, they were able to join the two spacecraft together during a space rendezvous, and they were also able to go on their first space walks outside of the spacecraft.

THE FIRST STEP ON THE MOON

After several years of test flights, experiments, and training, on July 16, 1969, the spacecraft known as Apollo 11 was launched in space. Included in the crew were astronauts Buzz Aldrin, Neil Armstrong and Michael Collins. It took three days to get to the moon.

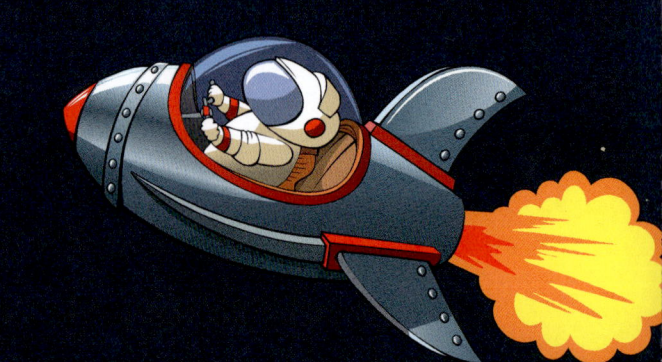

first step on the moon

Lunar Module Eagle

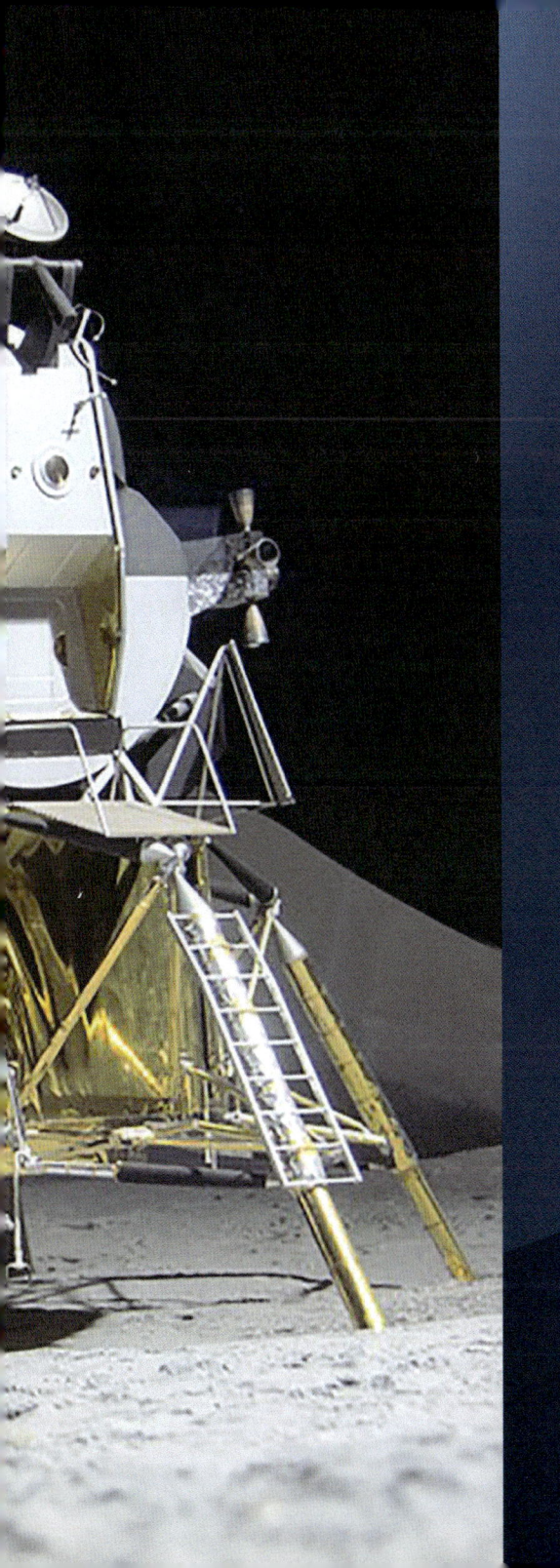

Once they arrived Buzz Aldrin and Neil Armstrong moved to the Eagle, which was the Lunar module, and started descending to the moon. After some malfunctions, Armstrong landed the module manually.

The Eagle landed on the moon on July 20, 1969. Once Neil Armstrong made his first step onto the moon, he announced "That's one small step for man, one giant leap for mankind."

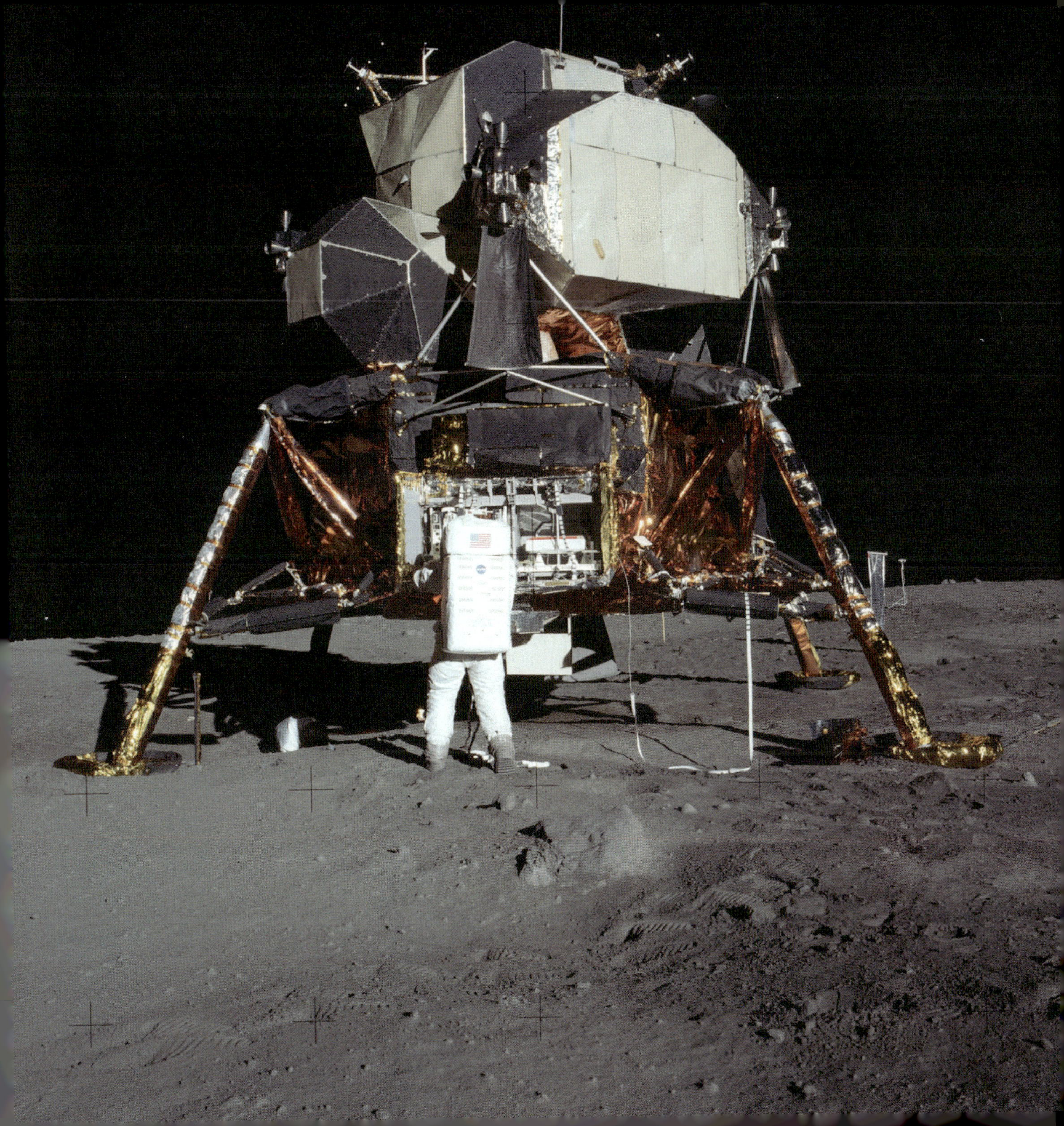

Apollo-Soyez project

THE END OF THE RACE

The United States had now taken a tremendous lead with the Gemini and the Apollo programs. Relations between the Soviet Union and the United States began to thaw in July of 1975 and the first joint US-Soviet mission took place known as the Apollo-Soyez project. The Space Race was officially over.

The Space Race was not without its failures and troubles. These included explosions and crashes, resulting in the deaths of several astronauts.

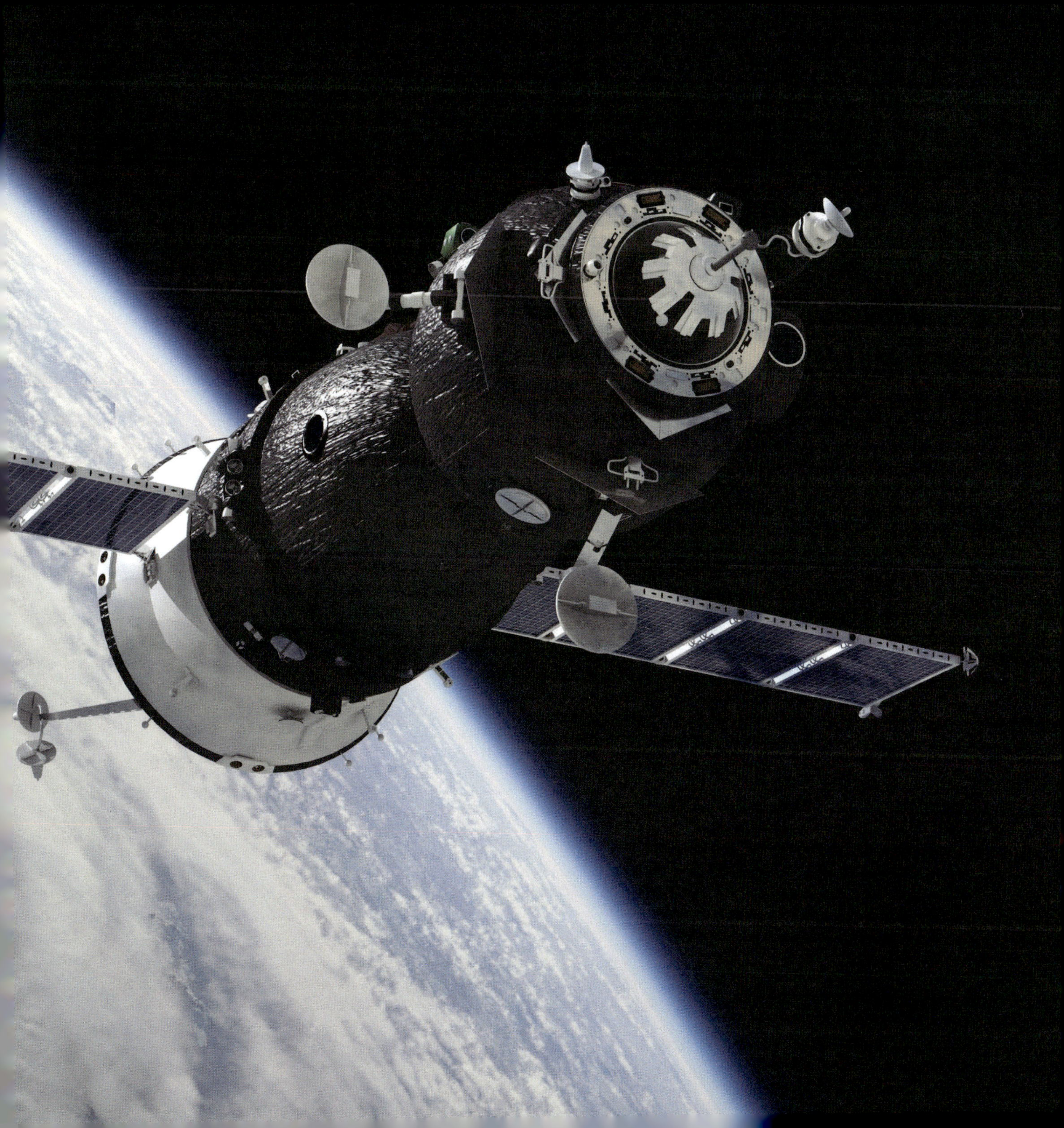

Apollo 13 space capsule

MOVING FORWARD

Once Apollo 11 had landed on the surface of the moon in July of 1969, six additional Apollo missions occurred by the end of 1972. During the Apollo 13 mission, the crew was able to somehow survive the explosion of an oxygen tank in the spacecraft's service module on their way to the moon.

THE SPACE SHUTTLE PROGRAM

Officially named the Space Transportation System (STS), the Space Shuttle Program was the United States' staffed launch vehicle program from 1981 until 2011. It was under the control of NASA (National Aeronautics and Space Administration) and officially began in 1972.

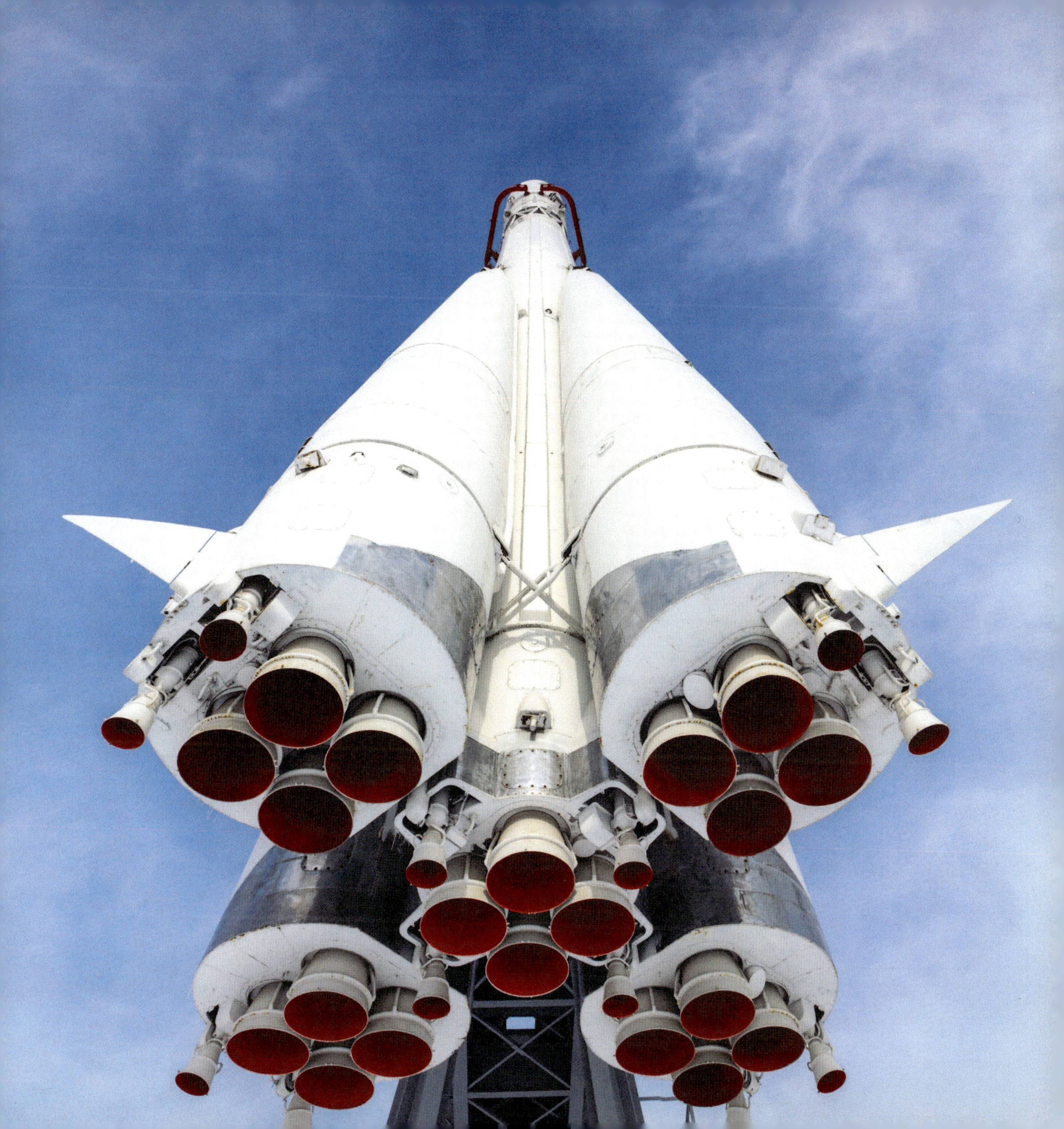

Orbiter

Composed of an orbiter, the space shuttle system was able to launch using two solid rocket boosters that were reusable, and an external fuel tank that was disposable. They were able to carry as many as eight astronauts, and 50,000 pounds of cargo into the LEO (low Earth orbit).

Upon completion of the mission, the obiter re-enters the Earth's atmosphere and lands in a way similar to a glider at either Edwards Air Force Base or the Kennedy Space Center.

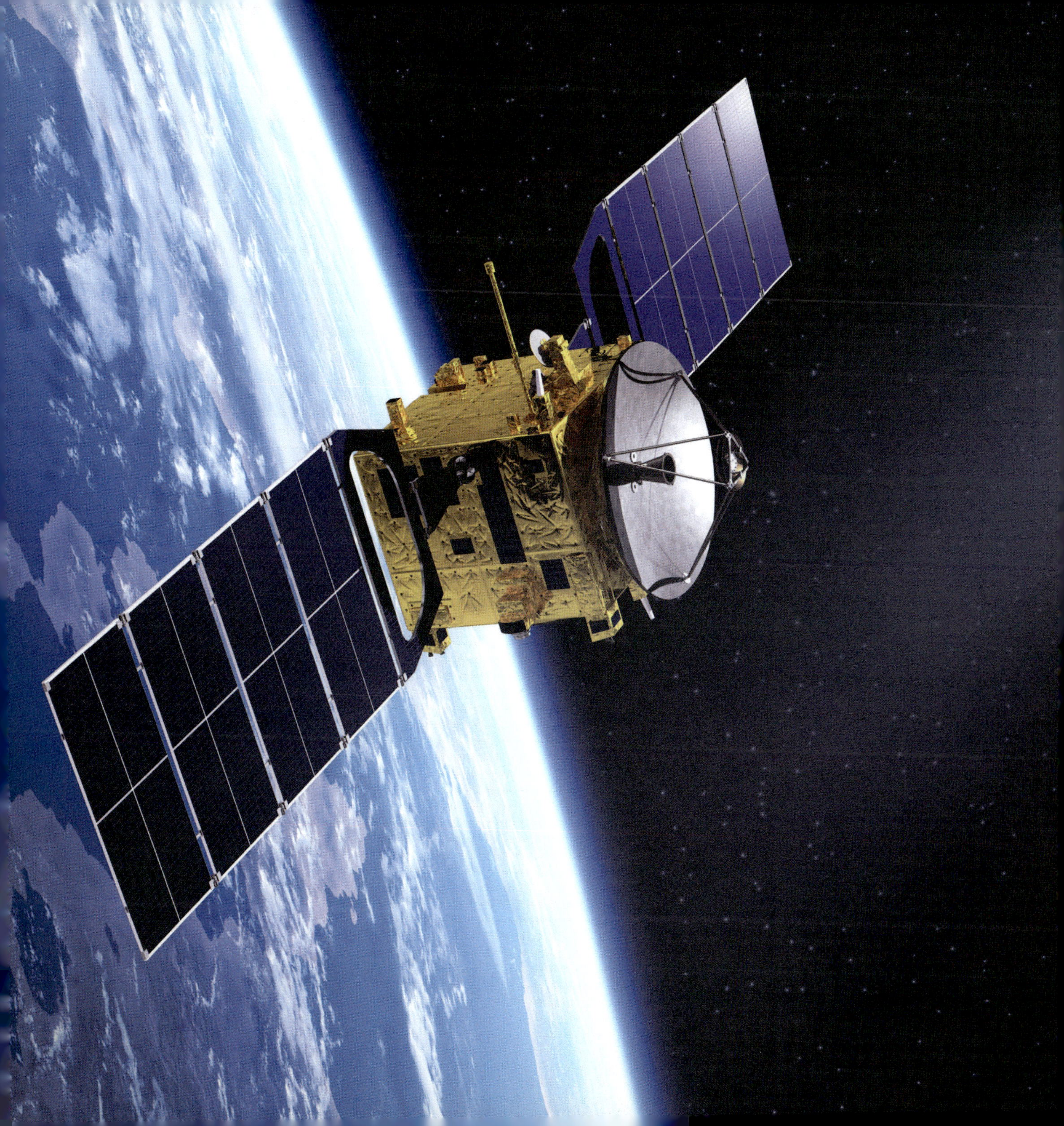

Columbia Space Shuttle

In 1981, the US launched Columbia, its first space shuttle. Eventually, 135 space missions were launched over the next 30 years.

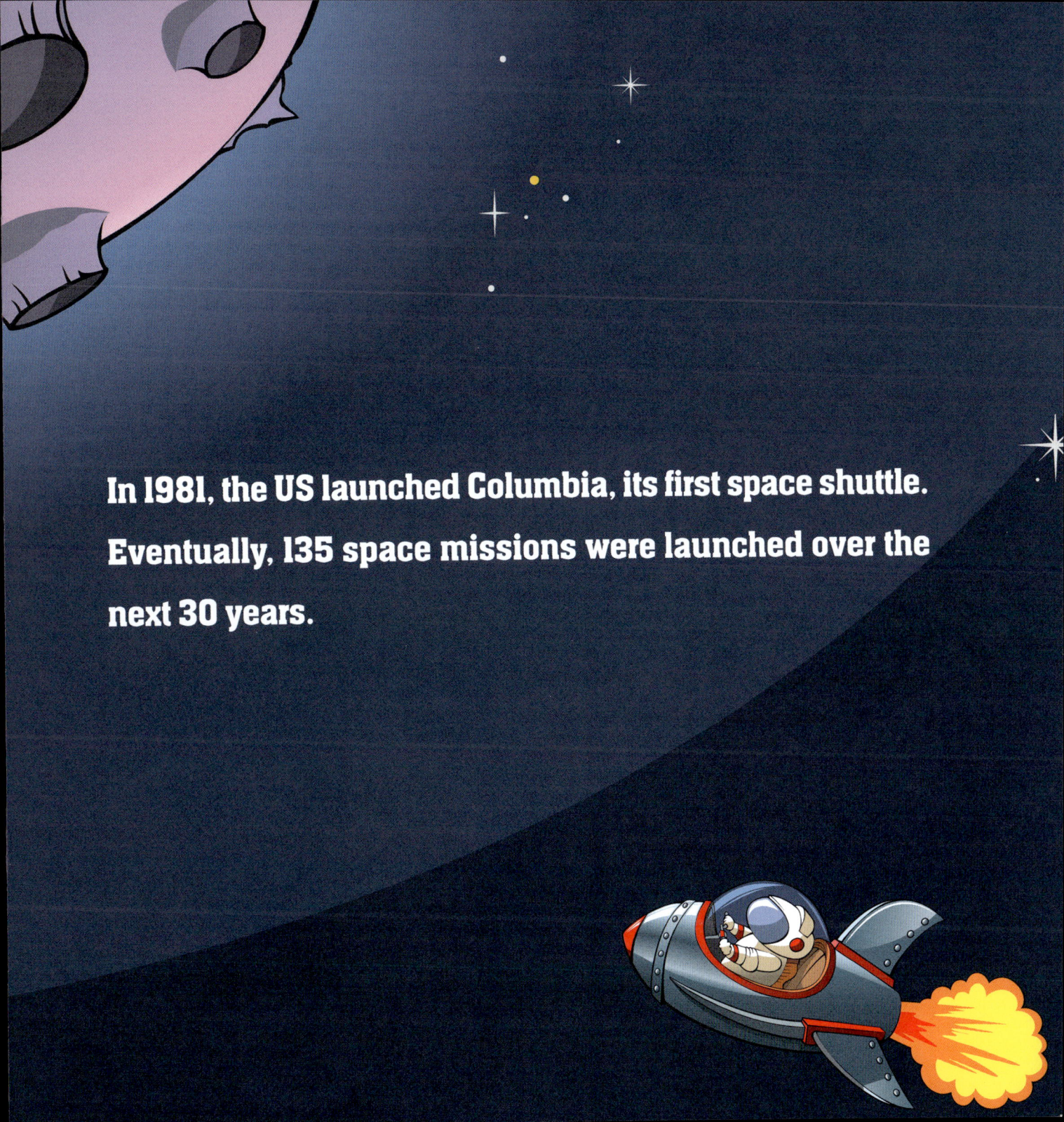

THE HUBBLE SPACE TELESCOPE

The Hubble Space Telescope (HST) is one of the most well-known telescopes. It was placed into orbit surrounding Earth in 1990 using the Space Shuttle and is still in operation. Since it is outside of the atmosphere of Earth, it is able to see outer space without any background light. This enables it to photograph some great pictures of galaxies and stars that are far away. The HST was named for the astronomer Edwin Hubble.

Hubble Space Telescope

Hubble Space Telescope

The Hubble is the only one that is intended to be serviced by the astronauts while in space. After its launch in 1990 by the Space Shuttle Discovery, five shuttle missions followed to repair, upgrade, and replace systems on it, including all of the five main instruments.

Following the Columbia disaster in 2003, NASA canceled the fifth mission for safety reasons. In 2009, the fifth servicing mission was approved and finally completed. As of 2017, the HST is still in operation and could remain in operation until 2030-2040. The James Webb Space Telescope (JWST), the scientific successor of the HST, is set for launch in 2018.

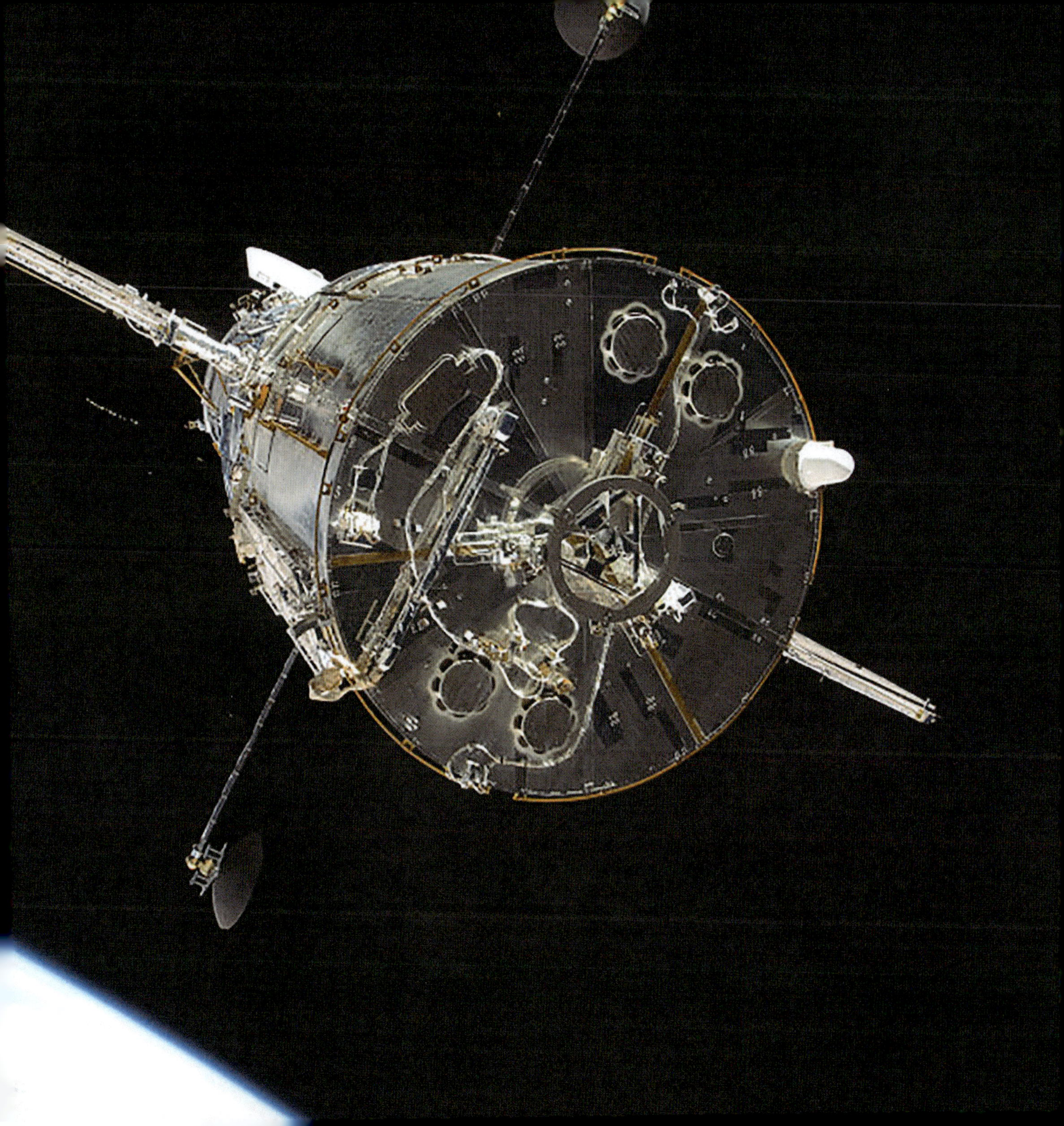

Space Shuttle Orbiting Earth

DISASTERS

The Space Shuttle Challenger broke apart after only 73 seconds on January 28, 1986 at 11:39 EST, and killed all seven of its crew members, consisting of five NASA astronauts and two payload specialists. It disintegrated above the Atlantic Ocean, which is located off the coast of Cape Canaveral, in Florida. The cause was determined to be the failure of an O-ring seal in the right solid rocket booster during liftoff.

The Space Shuttle Columbia disaster occurred February 1, 2003, when it disintegrated above Louisiana and Texas as it was re-entering the Earth's atmosphere, and killed all of its seven crew members. During its launch, a piece of the foam insulation broke away from its external tank and hit the orbiter on its left wing.

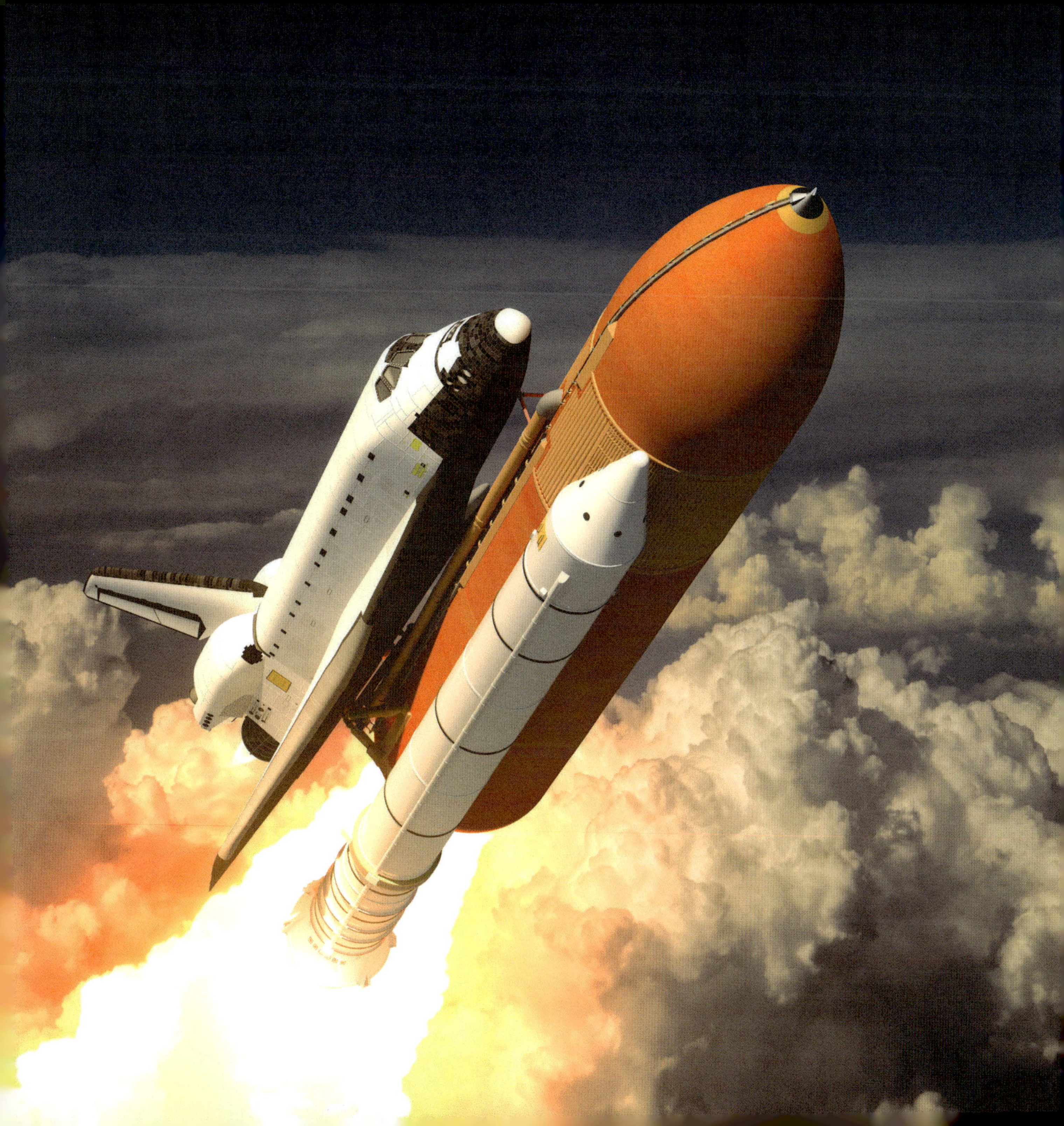

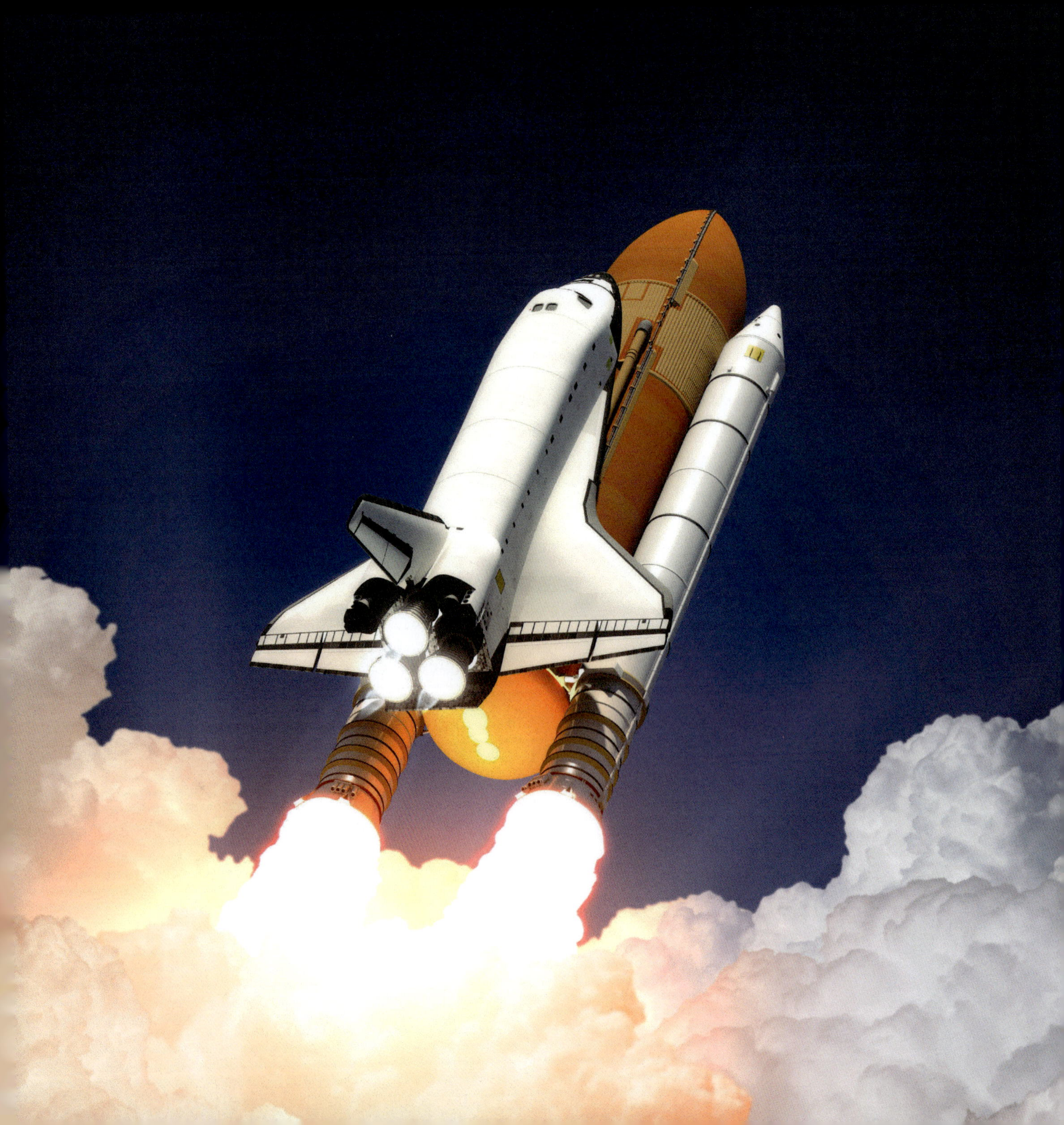

As it was re-entering the Earth's atmosphere, the damage that had been caused during the launch enabled hot atmospheric gases to enter into the wing structure, causing the spacecraft to become unstable and then break apart. After both of these disasters, Space Shuttle flights were suspended for over two years.

SPACE SHUTTLE RETIREMENT

Retirement of NASA's Space Shuttle fleet occurred between March 2011 and July 2011. The Space Shuttle Discovery was the first one to be retired, once it completed its last mission on March 9, 2011; Endeavor then followed and retired on June 1; and the Atlantis was the last shuttle mission completed, landing on July 21, 2011. This was the end of the Space Shuttle's 30-year program.

For additional information about space travel, you can go to your local library, research the internet and ask questions of your teachers, family and friends.

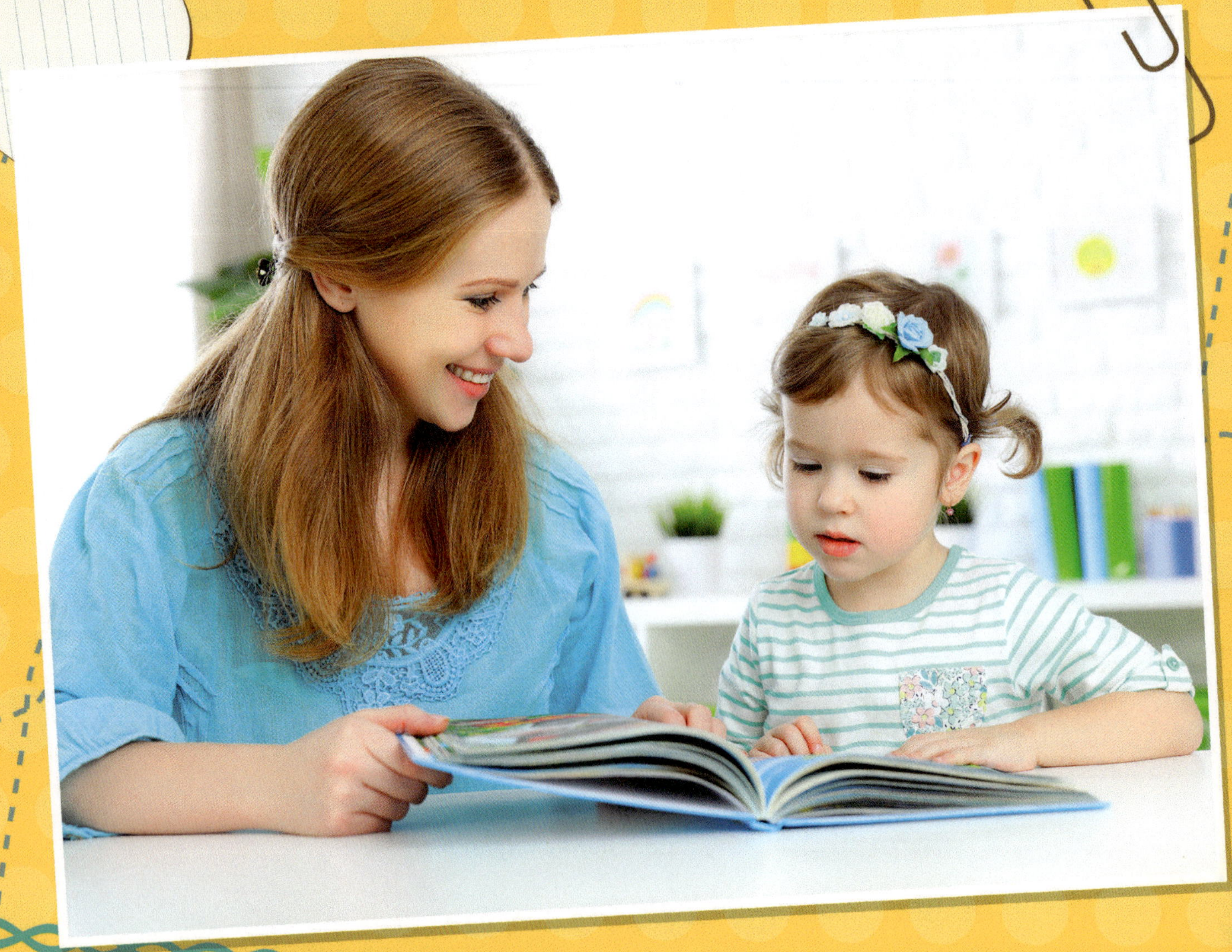

Visit

BABY PROFESSOR
EDUCATION KIDS

www.BabyProfessorBooks.com

to download Free Baby Professor eBooks and view our catalog of new and exciting Children's Books

Printed in Great Britain
by Amazon